THE POWER OF
NOW
HERE

DISCOVER THE POWER OF PRESENCE IN A DISTRACTED WORLD.

WRITTEN BY
MIKE JENSEN

LiveLifeHappy Publishing

Library of Congress Cataloging-in-Publication Data

Mike Jensen

The Power of NowHere. Choosing Presence in a Distracted World.

Self-Help / Personal Growth / Happiness / Body, Mind & Spirit / Inspiration & Personal Growth / Self-Help / Spiritual / Mindfulness & Meditation

ISBN: 978-1-998724-24-6 Paperback

ISBN: 978-1-998724-25-3 E-Book

Cover Design: Mike Jensen

Live Life Happy Publishing

PUBLISHER'S NOTE & AUTHOR DISCLAIMER

This publication is designed to provide accurate and authoritative information concerning the subject matter covered. It is sold to understand that the publisher and author are not engaging in or rendering any psychological, medical or other professional services. If expert assistance or counselling is needed, seek the services of a competent medical professional. For immediate support call your local crisis line. The following book could contain actual events and experiences that the author has encountered in their life. However, some names and specific locations have been changed or omitted to protect the privacy and confidentiality of the individuals involved. The changes do not alter the story's integrity or its messages.

Dedication:

To my clients—past, present, and future—who have ever said, "I feel like I'm going nowhere."

This book is for you.

You were never going nowhere. You were simply not NowHere.

Through our work together, I've watched you discover that the present moment is not empty—it's everything. It's the only place where life truly happens. From here, you've learned to release the weight of the past, quiet the noise of the future, and step into the influence you already carry.

This book is dedicated to those who have courageously embraced mindfulness and presence, transforming struggle into strength and confusion into clarity. It's also for those still in the midst of hardship, who feel lost or stuck. May these words remind you that you are not behind, you are not broken—you are simply being called back to the only moment that matters: NowHere.

TABLE OF CONTENT

INTRODUCTION

THE POWER OF NOWHERE

Most people I've worked with don't feel like they're living—
they feel like they're barely getting by. They say they feel lost.
Disconnected. Like they're going nowhere. I've heard that word
so many times from people in pain: Nowhere.

"I'm going nowhere in this job."

"My relationship is going nowhere."

"I feel like my life is just… stuck. Nowhere."

But here's the thing—nowhere is just one breath away from
something far more powerful. Shift your perspective and
look again:

Nowhere becomes Now Here.

That's not just clever wordplay—it's the truth most people miss.
We aren't really stuck in life… we're just absent from it. The
answers, the peace, the direction we keep searching for. They
don't exist in the past or some far-off future. They exist right
here, in the present. Always have. Always will.

But most of us are too distracted to notice. We're trapped
in mental loops, caught in reactive energy, trying to control

life instead of experiencing it. We scroll. We are numb. We think endlessly, but rarely pause to observe. And so we live disconnected—from others, from truth, and most importantly, from ourselves.

That's why I wrote this book. Not to teach some trendy version of mindfulness, but to remind you of what's always been available: your power lies in presence. Not in controlling everything around you, but in influencing how you show up. How you breathe. How you respond. How you reclaim your energy and re-enter your life.

You don't need a new destination—you need a new awareness of the ground you're already standing on.

This book is an invitation. An invitation to stop racing. To stop resisting. To stop thinking your life is "nowhere" when the truth is, it's Now Here, waiting for you to return to it.

So let's start. Let's wake up

Let's remember the power that was never gone—just forgotten.

CHAPTER 1

THE GREAT DISTRACTION

"You're not going nowhere—you're just not here yet. Presence isn't the escape. It's the way back home."

WHEN YOU'RE THERE,
BUT NOT REALLY THERE

Several years ago, I sat in a room full of people—but I wasn't really there.

I could hear the conversations. I nodded when someone spoke to me. I laughed at the right moments. But none of it reached me. I was like a shadow in the room—physically present, emotionally disconnected, spiritually drained. I was there, but I wasn't living. I was surviving in the space between regret and fear, stuck in my head, believing every lie that told me I wasn't enough, that I had no purpose, that I had failed too deeply to come back.

Back then, I didn't know what presence truly meant. I thought it was something reserved for peaceful people or monks on mountaintops. I had no idea that **presence is what saves you** when you feel like you're drowning. I didn't know that the very thing I was avoiding—the now—was the only place I could find healing, power, and peace.

Like so many others, I thought I was going nowhere. But the truth? I was just never *Now Here*.

That's where this begins.

We're All Distracted

Look around and you'll see a world running at full speed but going in circles. People wake up already stressed. They move through the day reacting, worrying, overthinking, trying to outrun the unease they feel but can't quite name. They scroll endlessly. Chase dopamine. Chase approval. Chase anything that will distract them from themselves.

We don't realize it, but distraction is the new addiction—and the worst part is, it's socially acceptable. It's praised. Being "busy" has become a badge of honor. Always doing, always achieving, always hustling. But what's the cost?

We've traded depth for speed.
Meaning for motion.
Awareness for anxiety.

And in the process, we've abandoned the only moment we ever actually have: **right now**.

Most people aren't afraid of being still because it's boring. They're afraid because it's *revealing*. In the silence, we meet ourselves. And when we've spent years distracting ourselves from truth, silence becomes uncomfortable—almost unbearable.

But that discomfort is the signal. It's not telling you to run—it's inviting you to return.

The Root of Disconnection

Distraction isn't just about technology or multitasking. It's much deeper than that. Distraction is the result of unresolved energy—unexamined beliefs, buried emotions, and unmet needs. It's how we cope when we don't know how to be.

When I was in that dark place—physically hurting, emotionally broken, mentally exhausted—I couldn't sit still. I couldn't be alone with my thoughts. I would distract myself with noise, substances, anything to not feel what I was feeling. I thought I was managing it. But I was avoiding it. And avoidance always prolongs pain.

Every time I ignored the present moment, I gave my power away. I allowed fear to drive the car. I let shame make my decisions. And every time I refused to face myself, I delayed my healing.

Presence didn't come to me in a bolt of lightning. It came in small, quiet moments when I couldn't run anymore. It came when I allowed the stillness to speak. When I finally chose to listen instead of escape. That's when everything changed—not instantly, but deeply.

From Reaction to Influence

Here's what I learned the hard way: if you are not present, you have lost your power—you are simply reacting. Life becomes something that *happens* to you, not something you participate in. You wake up exhausted, give your energy to people and problems that don't serve you, and wonder why you feel stuck.

But presence flips that entirely.

The moment you become aware, you reclaim your influence. Your power. You don't have to act like you control everything—you begin to **influence how you respond** to everything. And that one shift? That's where your power lives. That's where change begins.

You stop pouring energy into thoughts that don't serve you. You stop chasing validation that was never yours to begin with. You stop abandoning yourself in moments that matter most.

Presence doesn't promise a perfect life. But it does give you the clarity, strength, and awareness to live on purpose—even in pain.

The Truth About Now

The present moment is not just a nice idea—it's the only place where life actually exists. It's where healing happens. It's where connection happens. It's where you happen.

When you're present:
- You begin to notice the beauty in what you've overlooked.
- You stop overreacting to things that used to own your energy.
- You listen differently. Speak differently. Love differently.

Being present isn't about being passive. It's about becoming *fully* engaged with what is real. It's saying, "I may not know what's next, but I'm going to meet this moment with my full self."

Most people don't feel stuck because they're incapable—they feel stuck because they're absent. They're "nowhere" in their own lives, hoping something external will create internal change.

But here's the truth: **Your power isn't in a different place. It's in a different awareness**.

Coming Back to NowHere

This chapter isn't just a call to pay more attention. It's a wake-up call to stop abandoning the only place your life can truly change.

You're not going nowhere.
You've just forgotten to be Now Here.

This isn't about adding something new to your life—it's about subtracting what's been keeping you unconscious. It's about removing the static so you can hear what's been speaking to you all along.

The breath. The pause. The space. The whisper of intuition. The shift from reaction to reflection. From absence to awareness.

Presence is not a place you find—it's a place you return to.
And the door is always open.

REFLECTION QUESTIONS

1. Where in your life do you feel like you're "going no-where"? What's actually keeping you from being fully present in those areas?

2. What daily habits or distractions do you use to avoid stillness or discomfort?

3. Recall a recent moment when you felt fully present. What did it feel like? What made it possible?

4. How would your energy, relationships, or mindset shift if you made the present moment your home?

CHAPTER 2

YOU ARE NOT YOUR THOUGHTS

"Your thoughts are not the truth—they're noise dressed in your voice. Learn to hear them without obeying them."

WAKING UP FROM THE MIND GAME

I used to believe every thought that entered my mind.

If a thought told me I wasn't good enough, I accepted it. If it reminded me of my past failures, I relived them. If it projected fear into the future, I felt the anxiety immediately. There was no filter—no separation between what I thought and who I was. My mind ran the show, and I was just along for the ride.

Most people live like this without even realiing it. We're not thinking—we're being thought. And when we become fused with our thoughts, we stop being present. We lose clarity. We confuse noise with truth. We mistake mental chatter for divine wisdom. And over time, we become exhausted by trying to manage the emotional chaos created by a mind left unchecked.

But here's the truth I had to learn the hard way: **You are not your thoughts**.

That voice in your head? It's not the truth.
It's not your identity.
It's not your value.

It's just a stream of mental activity shaped by conditioning, belief systems, trauma, and fear.

You don't need to silence your mind—you need to stop identifying with it.

The Difference Between Thinking and Thought

There's a concept I teach in my work that changed everything for me:

Thinking is the conditioned, often fear-based inner dialogue you've been programmed to believe.

Thought—true thought—is intuitive, present, quiet, and often profound.

Thinking is reactive. Thought is reflective.
Thinking is noise. Thought is wisdom.
Thinking keeps you stuck in loops. Thought moves you toward clarity and peace.

Most people have never made this distinction. They hear a thought and take it as truth—without ever questioning where it came from, if it's even theirs, or if it serves any meaningful purpose.

Imagine if someone walked into your house, started shouting insults, and you just let them stay—fed them, gave them a bed, and let them make all your decisions. That's what most of us do with our thoughts. We give them full authority over our lives without ever asking, *"Do I actually believe this? Do I want this thought leading me?"*

You are not the thinker.
You are the one observing the thinking.

The Voice in Your Head Isn't Always Yours

Let's talk about where these thoughts even come from. Some come from past experiences. Some from culture. Some from your childhood. Some from fears that have been reinforced over time. Some aren't even yours—they're things you've heard or absorbed from other people and accepted without even realizing it.

That thought that says, *"I'll never be good enough,"* may have started with a teacher or parent or early failure—but it became your identity because you never challenged it.

That thought that says, *"I'm behind in life,"* might come from social media comparison or societal pressure—but it became your truth because you never paused to ask, "Behind according to who?"

We don't just live inside our minds—we often live inside the minds of those who influenced us.

The problem isn't that we have thoughts—it's that we believe them without investigation.

And belief is powerful. Because belief fuels emotion. Emotion fuels action. And action creates the results we experience.

The TEAR Method: How Thoughts Shape Reality

There's a model I teach called TEAR—and it illustrates exactly how this works.

T = Thoughts
E = Emotions
A = Actions
R = Results

Your thoughts create your emotional state.
Your emotions influence your behavior.
Your behavior determines your results.
And your results reinforce the original thought.

Let me give you a quick example.
Let's say you have a thought: *"I always mess things up."*
What emotion follows that? Shame. Guilt. Hopelessness.
What kind of action will that emotion lead to? Probably inaction—or self-sabotage.

And what's the result? You avoid trying, or you subconsciously fail... and reinforce the belief that you "always mess things up."

And the cycle continues.
But what if you interrupted that process?
What if you paused and asked: "Is that thought even true? *Who would I be without it?"*

That pause—that awareness—is where presence begins.

The Power of Observing, Not Absorbing

One of the most life-changing practices I ever adopted was this simple shift:

I started observing my thoughts instead of absorbing them.

When a limiting or negative thought came in, I would say to myself, *"There it is. That's not me—it's just a thought. I don't have to accept it."*

And over time, I started to regain power.
Not because I got rid of all my thoughts—because I stopped letting them define me.

You don't control what thoughts arise, but you do choose what energy you give them.
That is the essence of mindfulness.

Mindfulness isn't about controlling the mind. It's about **watching the mind with compassion and curiosity**. And once you watch something long enough, you realize it doesn't own you anymore.

The thoughts may still come—but they no longer lead.

A Personal Example: The Thought That Nearly Destroyed Me

During one of the darkest seasons of my life, a thought hit me that nearly broke me:

"You're a burden to everyone around you."

It felt so real, so convincing. And because I didn't know how to separate from it, I believed it. I began to isolate myself. I withdrew from family and friends. I stopped showing up in life because that one thought had become my identity.

But it wasn't true. It was a lie born from pain, exhaustion, and hopelessness.

Only when I began to sit with that thought—not run from it—did I discover it for what it was: a wounded belief looking for healing.

I had to ask: *What if this thought isn't the truth? What if I'm not a burden—but someone who's been carrying too much alone?*

That single shift—from identifying with the thought to questioning it—helped me begin my journey back into presence.

How to Begin Untangling From Your Thoughts

Start here:
- **Notice** the thought. Give it a name. ("There's the 'I'm not enough' story again.")

- **Pause** before reacting to it.

- **Question** it gently. Ask: Is this true? Is it helpful? Where did this come from?

- **Choose** what you want to believe instead. Anchor into a thought that empowers and aligns with your growth.

You're not trying to force positivity. You're trying to return to clarity.

Presence Is the Space Between Thought and Belief

Every moment you choose to *observe* instead of *identify*, you build the muscle of mindfulness. You strengthen your influence. You become less reactive and more intentional.

And the more often you choose presence, the more clearly you see:

You were never your thoughts.
You were always the observer.
You were always Now Here.

REFLECTION QUESTIONS

1. What is one recurring thought you tend to believe that causes you to feel stuck or small?

2. Where do you think that thought originated? Was it truly yours, or did it come from someone else's influence?

3. How does that thought affect your emotions, your actions, and the results you experience?

4. What would your life look like if you stopped identifying with that thought?

5. Can you begin to practice observing your thoughts today—without judgment, just curiosity?

CHAPTER 3

THE PRISON
OF REACTION

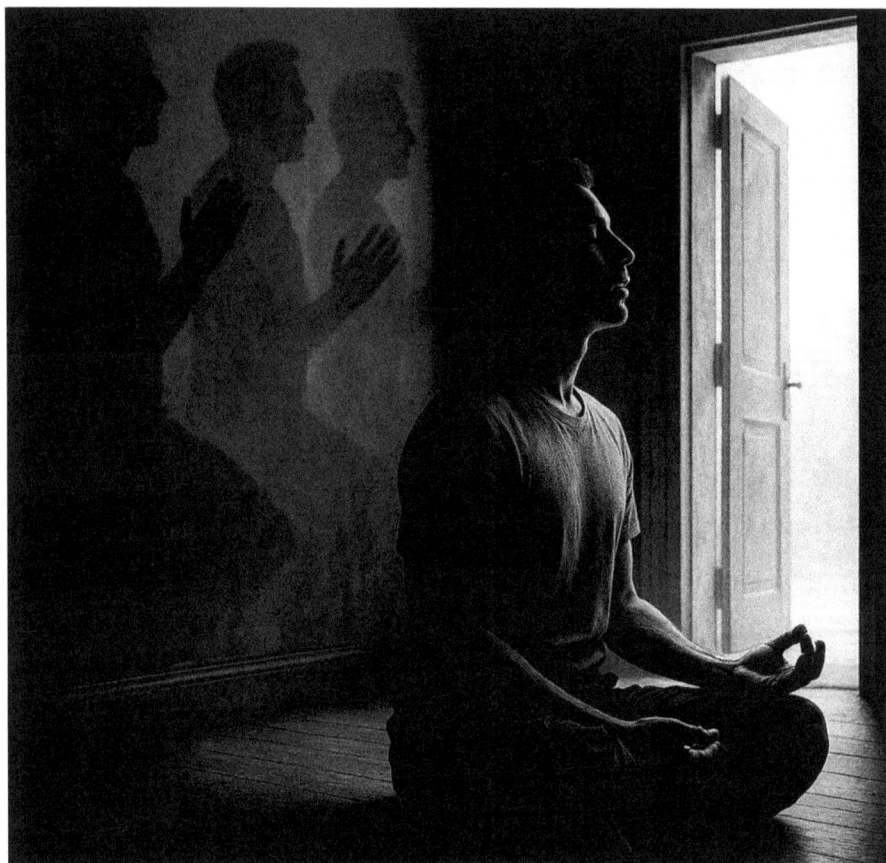

"Every reaction is a rehearsal of the past.
Every mindful breath is a doorway to freedom."

FROM AUTOMATIC TO AWARE

There's a pattern I've seen in almost every person I've coached. It doesn't matter their background, age, or profession. It's this: they feel like life keeps throwing them curveballs, and all they ever do is try to dodge them.

React. React. React.

It's as if they're caught in an endless game of emotional whack-a-mole—anger, stress, worry, guilt, regret—rising and falling like waves they can't control. They don't want to feel this way, but it keeps happening. And deep down, they're exhausted. But more than that, they're confused.

"Why do I keep doing this?"
"Why do I keep sabotaging myself?"
"Why do I always take the bait?"

The answer is simple, but rarely obvious when you're in the middle of it.

They're not present. They're reactive.
And when you're reactive, you're not choosing—you're surviving.

Living in Default Mode

Most of us live like we're on autopilot. Something happens, and we immediately respond with an emotion, a defense, or an escape route. We don't pause. We don't breathe. We don't check in with what's really happening—we just *go*.

Someone criticizes us. We get defensive.
Plans change suddenly? We panic.
Someone ignores us? We spiral into self-doubt.

But what's really happening underneath?

Most reactivity isn't about the moment in front of us—it's about **old programming**. It's rooted in past pain, limiting beliefs, unhealed wounds, and ego-driven fears. The present moment becomes distorted through the lens of past emotion.

We're not reacting to *what is*—we're reacting to what we *think it means*.

That's why reactivity keeps you trapped. It prevents presence. It hijacks your influence. It makes every moment about your past pain or your imagined future, and never about what's true *right now*.

My Own Trigger Trap

There was a time in my life when I couldn't get through a week—sometimes even a day—without getting triggered. I thought I had everything under control on the outside. But inside, I was walking on emotional landmines.

Something small could set me off. A comment. A delay. A failure to meet an expectation. I'd tell myself I was justified. I'd explain it away as stress. But if I was being honest, I was living in constant reaction—defending my identity, protecting my wounds, and trying to prove I had worth. It wasn't conscious, but it was consuming.

When I finally started paying attention, I saw the pattern. My nervous system was always braced for battle. My ego was always on guard. My thoughts were always trying to predict danger.

And in all that overreaction... I was never truly present.

It wasn't until I learned to **observe my reactions without obeying them** that something shifted. I realized I didn't have to respond to every emotion like it was truth. I didn't have to let the old story run my current life. And I didn't have to fight for control—I only needed to choose awareness.

The Pause is the Power

Here's the truth I wish more people understood:
You don't have to react.
You can pause. You can observe. You can influence.

That space between stimulus and response?
That's your freedom.
That's your power.
That's presence.

The ego loves immediacy. It wants to win the moment. It wants to defend, attack, or run. But the soul—the deeper part of you—it speaks in stillness. It doesn't rush. It doesn't shout. It waits for you to *come back to now.*

That's why I teach people to breathe before they speak. To step back before they step forward. To question their first instinct—not because it's always wrong, but because it's not always conscious.

The goal is not to suppress your emotions—it's to *witness them.* To feel fully, and still choose wisely.

From Catabolic to Anabolic Energy

Let's take this deeper with what I teach about energy. Reactions are typically **catabolic**—draining, destructive, and rooted in fear. They come from a place of needing to defend, prove, or protect.

Presence, on the other hand, allows for **anabolic** energy—constructive, creative, and rooted in clarity. It allows you to influence with awareness instead of manipulate from emotion.

Here's a simple way to tell the difference:

Catabolic reactions say: *I have no choice. This is just how I am.*

Anabolic responses say: *I have influence. I can choose a new way to show up.*

One leads to regret and repeated patterns.
The other leads to growth, freedom, and peace.

Breaking the Cycle

So how do we break free from reactivity and reclaim presence?

1. Recognize the Pattern - Start noticing your common triggers. What situations, people, or emotions tend to provoke automatic reactions in you? Write them down. Awareness is the first step to liberation.

2. Pause and Breathe - Even three conscious breaths can interrupt the emotional loop. This is not about denying how you feel—it's about creating enough space to *respond with clarity* instead of reacting from conditioning.

3. Question the Story - Ask: "What else could this mean?" Often, our reaction is based on an old belief or wound, not what's happening now. Challenge the assumptions behind your emotions.

4. Choose a Higher Energy Response - What would a response rooted in love, compassion, or self-respect look like? What would your most conscious self choose in this moment?
The more you practice, the more you'll find that your life starts to feel lighter—not because the circumstances change, but because *you're no longer a prisoner of your reactions.*

Your Influence Begins Now

If you remember anything from this chapter, let it be this:
You are not your reactions.
You are the one who sees them.
And that makes you powerful.

THE POWER OF NOWHERE

When you stop reacting automatically, you start
influencing intentionally.
You return to the moment, to yourself, to presence.
And in that space, everything begins to shift.

You're no longer the puppet. You're the chooser.
You're no longer "nowhere." You're **Now Here**—and fully awake.

REFLECTION QUESTIONS

1. What are the three most common triggers that cause
   you to react unconsciously? How do those reactions
   usually show up?

2. When was the last time you reacted emotionally and
   regretted it? What belief or fear might have fueled
   that reaction?

3. What does the "pause" look like for you? How can
   you create more space between what happens and how
   you respond?

4. In what areas of life would shifting from reaction to
   influence make the biggest difference for your peace,
   clarity, or growth?

34

CHAPTER 4

THE MOMENT IS THE ONLY DOOR

"The future you're chasing and the past you're replaying both dissolve in the presence of now."

THE ENTRYWAY TO EVERYTHING YOU'RE SEEKING

You've heard the phrase "Be here now" a hundred times.
It's written on coffee mugs and yoga mats.
But how often do we truly grasp the power of that phrase—not as a trendy mantra, but as a way of life?

I didn't.

For a long time, I thought being present meant I was just supposed to breathe and ignore my problems. That it was a luxury reserved for people without stress, trauma, or a million responsibilities. But presence isn't about ignoring life—it's about engaging with it **fully and consciously**, especially when it's hard.

Presence is **not** passive.
It's not a bypass or escape.
It's a position of strength. Of grounded power. Of influence.

And the moment I began to understand that, something inside me shifted.

Your Life Only Exists in One Place

We spend most of our lives anywhere but here.
We relive past mistakes.
We rehearse future problems.
We imagine conversations, replay arguments, create mental stories that may never even happen. And we wonder why we're so drained.

But think about it: **everything real only ever happens now.**
Your past? It's a memory—an echo of energy.
Your future? A projection—imagined scenarios that may never play out.

But your presence—right now, this breath, this awareness—is the only place anything actually happens. It's the only place healing occurs, relationships connect, and decisions carry power.

The moment is the only door. Miss it, and you miss the opportunity to change.

I Used to Live Everywhere But Now

I remember vividly when I first started to practice this truth. I was sitting outside, still carrying emotional pain and resentment from the past, still terrified about my future. I looked around and realized I couldn't actually enjoy anything in front of me. Not the air, the sun, or even my own body's stillness. I was there—but I wasn't **here.**

I was full of worry, anger, regret—fighting battles in my head that didn't even exist anymore. And that's when it hit me: I can't change the past. I can't live in the future. And right now, this *very moment*, I have a choice:

Be present—or stay a prisoner.

That one insight didn't solve everything overnight, but it *opened the door*. A door I didn't even know existed until I stopped looking for something *out there* to save me.

The Mind is Loud—Presence is Quiet

One of the greatest challenges to being present is that the mind is **never quiet on its own**. It's always narrating, labeling, judging, solving. It wants to protect you, yes, but it often ends up hijacking your ability to *experience* life in real time.

Your mind says:
- "Why did I say that yesterday?"
- "What if this doesn't work out?"
- "I have to figure out what to do next…"

But your presence?

It says:
- "I'm breathing."
- "I'm safe in this moment."
- "Let's respond with clarity."

That's why mindfulness isn't about becoming thoughtless. It's about becoming *aware of the thinker*—and choosing not to let it run the show.

It's about being the observer of your experience without immediately reacting to it. That space between stimulus and response? That's your power. That's where transformation begins.

Stop Waiting for a Better Moment

We convince ourselves that *this* moment isn't the one that matters.

We say things like:
- "When I get that promotion, then I'll slow down."
- "When my relationship improves, I'll finally feel better."
- "Once I have more time, I'll focus on myself."

But all of that is a trap.

Waiting for the perfect moment is how people waste their lives. The truth is, *now* is all we've ever had. If you can't find peace here, you won't find it anywhere else either.

You don't heal by escaping this moment—you heal by *entering it fully*.

You don't grow by waiting for life to change—you grow by showing up *before* it does.

Presence isn't what happens *after* your life improves. It's what causes your life to improve.

Accessing the Now: A Simple Practice

Here's a practice I use with my clients when they feel over-whelmed or disconnected. I call it **"3 to Return."**

Wherever you are, whatever is going on, pause and do three things:

1. **Breathe deeply** – Not to "fix" your feelings, but to reconnect with your body. Let the breath remind you that you are alive, and that's enough.

2. **Notice your surroundings** – Use your senses. What do you see? Hear? Smell? Feel on your skin? Anchor yourself in what's *real*, not what's imagined.

3. **Choose one thing to influence** – Ask: "What energy do I want to bring into this moment?" Whether it's calm, focus, gratitude, or compassion—**choose your presence**.

This isn't about perfection. It's about *pattern interruption*. It's about training yourself to return to now without judgment.

Real-Life Example: A Coaching Breakthrough

A client of mine was spiraling in anxiety—caught in a storm of "what ifs." He'd lost his job and kept saying, "I just feel like I'm falling behind. Everyone else is moving forward. I'm stuck."

I asked him one question: "What's happening in this moment that's actually wrong?"

He paused. Looked around. "Well… nothing really. I'm safe. My bills are paid this month. I just don't know what's next."

And that's where the work began.

We practiced returning to the present moment—not to deny his fears, but to **neutralize their grip**. The job loss didn't define him. The story about failure did. When he stayed in *this moment*, he found space. And in that space, new clarity arrived. New ideas. New motivation. All because he walked through the only door that exists: *NOW*.

You Are the Doorway

Here's what I need you to hear:
- You are not waiting for a moment—you *are* the moment.
- You are not missing an opportunity—you are standing inside of it.
- You are not stuck—you are simply uncentered.

And the good news? That can change.

You don't need to figure out everything.
You don't need to eliminate every distraction.
You just need to return to now—again and again—until presence becomes your home.

This is how you go from "nowhere" to *Now Here*. Not by adding more—but by returning to what's already within you.

REFLECTION QUESTIONS

1. In what areas of your life do you find yourself waiting for a "better" moment instead of showing up for the one you're in?

2. What internal or external distractions pull you away from presence the most?

3. How do you typically respond to stillness or silence? Why?

4. Practice "3 to Return" once today. What shifted in your body, thoughts, or energy?

5. What would it mean for you to fully inhabit this moment—not tomorrow, not someday, but *now*?

CHAPTER 5

THE ILLUSION
OF CONTROL

"The more you try to control life, the more it controls you. Awareness doesn't change the moment. It changes you—and that changes everything."

LETTING GO TO TAKE BACK YOUR POWER

There was a time in my life when I thought control was every-thing. If I could just control my environment, my emotions, outcomes, and the people around me, then I'd finally have peace. I thought I'd feel safe. I thought I'd feel enough. But here's the truth—control gave me nothing but stress, anxiety, frustration, exhaustion, and constant disappointment. I tried to bend life into something predictable, and when it refused to cooperate, I felt powerless and ashamed. My obsession with control was just fear in disguise.

Eventually, I learned: control is an illusion. You can't control other people's opinions, reactions, or choices. You can't control outcomes. You can't control the past or prevent every hardship in the future. What you can influence—that's where your real power lives. That influence begins the moment you choose to be present.

Presence is not passive; it's active awareness. It's seeing things as they are and realizing that your strength lies not in forcing the world to bend but in how you navigate its twists and turns.

When you begin to accept this, you start shifting from exhaustion to empowerment.

The Fear Beneath the Illusion

We don't chase control because we're broken; we chase it because we're afraid. Control becomes our shield and our false security blanket. When life hurts us—when chaos knocks us down, when uncertainty makes us feel small—we naturally want something to hold onto. The mind whispers: "If I can just control everything, I won't get hurt again."

But how's that working out? Control doesn't bring peace—it brings pressure. It doesn't eliminate pain—it prolongs it. It doesn't reduce suffering—it creates more of it. And worst of all, it pulls us out of the present moment. When you're trying to control everything, you're no longer available to experience anything.

Think of moments where fear dictated your actions—times you planned every word in a conversation or rehearsed every possible outcome. Did it ever truly ease your fear, or did it build even more tension inside you? Recognizing this cycle is the first step toward breaking it.

The Cost of Control

Control is seductive. It gives us a false sense of safety. For a while, it feels like it works. But at what cost? We overthink until our peace is gone. We micromanage relationships until they suffocate. We obsess over planning every detail and miss the moment we're in. We try to fix or save people instead of accepting them as they are. We demand life go our way, and when it doesn't, we spiral.

Imagine a parent trying to control every aspect of their teenager's life—grades, friends, hobbies. Instead of fostering a loving, open relationship, that control breeds resentment and rebellion. The parent feels misunderstood while the teen feels trapped. If the parent shifted from control to influence—communicating openly, leading by example, allowing natural consequences— the dynamic would completely change.

Control kills spontaneity, connection, curiosity, playfulness, and even joy. It places walls around opportunities for growth and keeps us stuck in fear. Fear thrives in uncertainty and feeds on "what ifs." Living in fear prevents us from truly living in the present.

My Breaking Point With Control

During the darkest stretch of my life, I had a broken back, a lost career, and a mind flooded with fear and hopelessness. I tried desperately to control everything—my pain, my circumstances, the way people saw me, even the way I felt. I thought managing it all would save me. But control suffocated me. It kept me reactive, angry, and exhausted. It kept me from being present with my family, myself, and my life.

What changed wasn't a master plan—it was the moment I let go. Not gave up—let go. I stopped micromanaging the world and started observing what was happening within me. I shifted from controlling outcomes to focusing on how I showed up. That shift—from control to presence—is when healing began.

That moment taught me resilience isn't about dominating life's challenges—it's about showing up despite them. It's learning to navigate uncertainty with courage and self-awareness.

Influence vs. Control

You don't need control to feel powerful. You need influence. Influence isn't about bending the world to your will. It's about managing your internal world so you can respond with clarity and wisdom—no matter what's happening externally.

Control says: "Nothing can go wrong." Influence says: "Even if it does, I choose who I become."

Control says: "I must fix everything." Influence says: "I lead through energy, not force."

Control says: "If I think hard enough, I'll figure it out." Influence says: "Clarity comes from stillness, not panic."

Consider an athlete trying to control every outcome in a game—they tighten up, overthink, and lose flow. Contrast that with an athlete who focuses on influencing their mindset and energy. They trust their training, adapt in real-time, and stay present. That's the power of influence.

Living from influence anchors you in awareness—not in the outcome. You're no longer trying to steer the storm; you're learning to stand in it, calmly and consciously. That's presence. That's power. That's freedom.

Presence Exposes the Illusion

You can't be present and controlling at the same time. Presence requires surrender and trust. Trust is terrifying for someone who's built safety around control. But this is where transformation begins.

When I slowed down, paused, and observed, I saw how much energy I wasted forcing things. I saw how tightly I held expectations and how afraid I was of vulnerability. I saw that nothing I tried to control ever gave me peace—not once. The moment I accepted the present, something shifted. I found space, clarity, and power—not over others, but within myself. That's the gift of presence.

Imagine a teacher releasing control and allowing students to explore ideas freely. Suddenly, creativity flourishes, and deeper learning occurs. Presence is that release—it allows life's natural rhythm to teach us instead of fighting against it.

Real-Life Applications: Conversations and Chaos

I once faced a difficult conversation I had avoided for years. I scripted every word, imagined every response, and convinced myself that control would determine success. When the day came, I abandoned the script. I led with presence, grounded and calm. I didn't manipulate or convince. I spoke truthfully and openly.

The conversation wasn't perfect, but I walked away in peace. I didn't control it—I influenced it through presence. That was enough.

Another client—a high-level executive—came to me after a major deal collapsed. He spiraled, losing sleep and replaying events. He thought doubling down on control was the solution. His breakthrough came when he paused, felt his emotions, and reconnected with the moment. When his energy shifted, his decisions improved. That's influence over reaction.

Think of a classroom teacher who insists on controlling every word and movement of their students. The classroom feels tense, creativity is stifled, and learning stalls. A teacher who lets go of control and focuses on influencing through encouragement and guidance sees students thrive because they feel trusted and understood.

Tools for Letting Go

- **Awareness Check:** Ask yourself, "Is this within my control or just my influence?"

- **Pause and Breathe:** Give space for clarity instead of rushing to fix.

- **Shift Language:** Replace "I need to control" with "I can influence."

- **Anchor in Now:** Notice what's true in this moment without projecting future fear.

- **Respond, Don't React:** Choose actions aligned with your values rather than fear.

- **Reflect Daily:** Write down one area each day where you successfully influenced rather than tried to control.

Practice these steps regularly, and you'll see your stress diminish and your relationships deepen. The more you engage with these tools, the more natural letting go becomes.

What Letting Go Really Means

Letting go isn't resignation. It's saying: "I'm done wasting energy on what I was never meant to control."

It's releasing your grip on what's out there and returning to what's in here.

Stop obsessing over opinions.
Stop demanding perfection.
Stop replaying the past.

Picture someone white-knuckling a steering wheel during a storm. The tension doesn't stop the rain—it only adds exhaustion. Letting go doesn't mean abandoning the car; it means loosening the grip, trusting your skills, and driving with calm focus.

Anchor yourself in now. Show up fully. Influence your energy. Choose your response. Slowly, life shifts—not because you forced it, but because you aligned with it.

You Were Never Meant to Control It All

You're not designed to control the world. You're designed to respond with wisdom. Real mastery isn't controlling the external but stewarding your internal state. You can only do that in one place: Now. Here.

This Moment is Enough

Life will always have moments that feel chaotic—loss, endings, changes. Trying to control those moments deepens suffering. But presence allows you to be steady even when the ground shakes.

Everything you need for your next best moment is already Now Here. You don't need to know tomorrow's outcome or fix every problem today. You don't need to control what's out of reach.

Just ask: What can I influence right now with who I am and how I show up?

That's where power and peace live. That's the invitation of presence.

REFLECTION QUESTIONS

1. Where are you trying to control something or someone? How is that impacting your peace?

2. Which anxieties are truly within your influence?

3. How might your energy shift if you chose presence over fear?

4. What belief about control are you ready to challenge today?

5. How would relationships or career look different if you led with influence instead of control?

CHAPTER 6

TRAINING THE OBSERVER

"You can't master your life until you meet the one who's watching it unfold—you."

THE PRACTICE OF WATCHING WITHOUT JUDGMENT

For most of my life, I reacted to everything.
Someone said something I didn't like? I responded defensively.
A situation didn't go my way? I spiraled into frustration or self-doubt.
I was a walking reaction—a man convinced he was making conscious decisions, when in reality I was letting old beliefs, unhealed wounds, and unconscious habits run my life.

It wasn't until I discovered the **observer** within me that things began to change.

That shift didn't come easily. In fact, it felt impossible at first. How do you observe your own thoughts when you're drowning in them? How do you step outside your emotions when they feel so immediate and consuming?

The answer is simple—but not easy: **You practice.**
You practice awareness the same way you practice a muscle.
You train yourself to witness instead of react. To see what's happening without becoming it.

You Are Not the Story

Most people live in a constant state of inner noise—narratives about who they are, what others think, what might happen next. These stories aren't neutral; they're fueled by emotion and past experience. And because we're not trained to question them, we believe every word.

The problem is, most of those stories aren't true.
They're **interpretations**, not facts.
And unless we learn to observe those interpretations, we become trapped inside them.

This is why training the observer is so powerful. When you become the watcher of your thoughts instead of the prisoner of them, you stop reacting blindly. You start choosing how to respond. You start *influencing* your experience instead of being owned by it.

It's the difference between being stuck in a storm and watching the weather pass from shelter. One feels chaotic and endless. The other? Safe, calm, clear.

The Observer is Always Present

Presence isn't just about feeling peaceful or focused. It's about stepping into the role of **observer**—that quiet, steady awareness behind the noise.

You've already experienced this, even if you didn't know what to call it.

Have you ever had a moment where you *caught yourself* about to say something reactive and paused instead? That's your observer.

Have you ever sat in silence and suddenly noticed the endless chatter happening inside your head? That's your observer.

Have you ever realized mid-conversation that your emotions were about to take over, but chose to stay grounded? That's your observer.

The observer isn't some mystical thing. It's the real you—the part of you that exists beyond your stories, beyond your ego, beyond your fears. It's the one who watches it all without getting lost in any of it.

And the more you practice becoming that presence, the more powerful and peaceful you become.

The Practice: Awareness Without Judgment

Here's the trap most people fall into: they begin to observe, but then they judge what they see.

"I shouldn't be thinking this."
"Why do I always feel this way?"
"I thought I was past this by now."

But judgment is just another layer of thought.
It's ego disguised as growth.
And it keeps you just as stuck as ignorance does.

True observation is **nonjudgmental awareness**. It's seeing your thoughts, emotions, and patterns exactly as they are, without trying to fix, fight, or explain them. It's saying: "This is what's here right now," and letting that be enough.

This kind of awareness is revolutionary. Because once you see something clearly, you can finally begin to release it.

My Personal Turning Point

There was a morning—after a particularly rough night—where I sat on the edge of my bed and didn't try to "do" anything. I didn't try to fix my emotions or escape them. I just *watched* them. I let them rise. I let them be.

And for the first time in a long time, I felt a sense of stillness that I hadn't known was possible.

It didn't mean my life changed instantly. But that morning was the first time I met myself with complete presence. I didn't feel ashamed of what I felt. I didn't pretend to be stronger than I was. I just observed—and in that observation, something shifted.

That moment taught me that I had more influence than I thought. Not over the world. Not over other people. But over how I met myself.

The Power of the Pause

One of the simplest and most profound ways to train the observer is through the practice of *pausing*.

Before reacting to a situation, pause.
Before responding to a triggering thought, pause.
Before spiraling into fear or judgment, pause.

That pause is your access point. It's the space where awareness lives. And it's the gap where transformation begins.

In the pause, ask:
- "What am I feeling right now?"
- "What belief or story is driving this reaction?"
- "Is this energy I want to bring into the moment?"

This isn't about overthinking or analyzing. It's about creating enough space for presence to return.

Real-Life Example: Coaching the Observer

I once worked with a client named Mark who constantly battled anger in his relationships. Every disagreement triggered a deep emotional storm. He'd lash out, then feel ashamed afterward. His story was that he had a "bad temper" and couldn't change.

But when we began to train his observer, everything shifted.

Instead of trying to suppress his anger, I encouraged him to witness it. When he felt the heat rising, I had him pause, breathe, and simply observe: "Where is this in my body? What thoughts are present? What does this emotion believe it's protecting?"

Over time, Mark stopped reacting blindly. He started responding with awareness. He wasn't less emotional—he was **more**

conscious. And as a result, his energy shifted. His relationships improved. And for the first time, he felt proud of how he showed up.

That's the power of observation.

You Can't Change What You Won't Face

Most people want to change their lives, but they're unwilling to face themselves first. They want freedom, but they're not willing to sit still long enough to recognize their inner prison.

But here's the truth:
You can't influence what you haven't observed.
You can't release what you refuse to acknowledge.
And you'll never live fully present if you keep running from the parts of yourself that need your awareness most.

Training the observer is not about becoming perfect—it's about becoming real. It's about meeting every part of yourself with compassion, curiosity, and courage.

This is your practice now.
Not fixing. Not fighting.
Just watching.
And choosing with intention instead of reacting with habit.

REFLECTION QUESTIONS

1. What are some recurring thoughts or emotional patterns you've noticed in your daily life?

2. In what situations do you find yourself reacting unconsciously? What triggers you?

3. How do you typically judge yourself when uncomfortable thoughts or emotions arise?

4. What might change if you replaced that judgment with gentle observation?

5. What would it look like to pause more often and choose your response instead of reacting?

CHAPTER 7

ENERGY FIRST, ACTION SECOND

"Before you speak, decide. Before you act, breathe.
Energy is the message—action is just the echo."

INFLUENCE IS FOUND IN THE ENERGY YOU BRING

We're trained to act. To hustle. To solve problems. To take charge and make something happen. And while action matters—don't get me wrong—most people are skipping the most important step.

Before any meaningful action comes something far more powerful: **energy.**

In every conversation, interaction, or decision, there's a silent force at play: the energy behind it. You've felt this before, even if you didn't name it. You've walked into a room where something "felt off." You've talked to someone who said the right words, but something about them didn't sit right. You've probably made decisions that "looked" smart on paper—but didn't feel aligned in your body. That's not coincidence. That's energy.

And here's the truth most people miss:
Your energy speaks louder than your actions.

What Energy Are You Bringing?

Energy is the invisible language of life. It communicates your mindset, your emotions, your intentions—*before you ever open your mouth.* If you're rushing into action with frustration, fear, or desperation driving the wheel, your results will reflect that. Maybe not immediately, but always eventually.

On the other hand, when your energy is grounded, centered, and anabolic—meaning creative, loving, and present—your actions carry a different weight. They become magnetic. Impactful. Clear.

This is why presence matters so much. It's not just about feeling peaceful—it's about aligning your internal state before you engage with the world. Because when you don't, you end up:

- Overreacting and regretting it
- Making decisions based on fear instead of faith
- Saying yes when you should say no
- Trying to fix things that don't need fixing
- Exhausting yourself trying to control what's not yours to control

Sound familiar?

I know it does—because I lived like that for years.

When I Let Energy Lead

There was a time when I believed my value was in what I did. I would rush into solving problems—whether mine or someone else's—because action gave me a false sense of control. If I could fix it, I felt useful. But I didn't realize that I was constantly reacting. I wasn't leading with awareness. I wasn't grounded.

And I wasn't actually helping—I was just temporarily managing the chaos I helped create by moving too fast.

It wasn't until I started pausing—really pausing—to feel where my energy was coming from that everything changed. I began to ask different questions:

"Is this coming from love or fear?"
"Am I trying to prove something or serve something?"
"Is this action aligned with who I am—or who I'm trying to impress?"

Those questions slowed me down. They made me uncomfortable at first. But they also gave me back my influence. I began to notice that when I acted from a clear, present, mindful place, life responded differently. People did too. My words landed differently. My decisions created more peace than damage. And I stopped chasing the illusion of control.

The Frequency of Influence

Think of your energy like a radio frequency. If you're tuned to chaos, anxiety, or people-pleasing, that's what you'll transmit—and attract. If you're tuned to groundedness, clarity, and inner confidence, your world responds in kind.

This isn't spiritual fluff. It's real. **Everything is energy**—your thoughts, your tone, your intentions. The way you walk into a room or speak to a loved one matters. People *feel* you before they hear you. The more conscious you become of that, the more intentional you can be in everything you do.

Let me be clear—this isn't about perfection. It's about **alignment**. You'll still get angry. You'll still feel fear. You'll still want to act quickly at times. That's human. The key is not to let those emotions be the fuel for your choices.

Pause. Breathe. Center. Then act.

The moment you do, you shift from being **reactive** to being **responsive**—and that's where your real power lives.

Practical Tools to Shift Energy

You don't need hours of meditation or a silent retreat to change your energy. You just need a moment of awareness and a willingness to shift. Here are tools I personally use and coach others through:

1. The Energy Check-In: Before any important conversation, meeting, or decision—ask yourself:
- "What energy am I carrying right now?"
- "Is this how I want to show up?"
- "What's influencing me—fear, ego, love, clarity?"

Awareness is the first shift.

2. The Breath Reset: Three deep breaths. That's it. It sounds simple, but it's a powerful interrupter of anxious or reactive energy. It brings your attention back to your body and resets your nervous system.

3. Delay the Action: Not everything needs to be handled *right now*. When you feel urgency or pressure, ask: "Is this urgent—

or am I uncomfortable with stillness?" If possible, wait an hour. Let your energy settle, and then respond.

4. Write Before You Speak: If emotions are high, write down what you want to say first. It gives the reactive energy time to dissipate and lets your words come from influence, not impulse.

Why This Matters in Presence

Every moment is an opportunity to either **react or respond**. Reactivity pulls you out of the present—it makes you serve your emotions rather than master them. But a mindful response *comes from presence*. It means you're grounded in who you are, not just what you feel.

Energy is the *bridge* between presence and action.

If you've ever said or done something and then immediately regretted it, you've seen what happens when energy leads the wrong way. But when you pause, feel, and choose your response with intention, that's how you lead your life. That's how you influence outcomes without ever needing to control them.

The Power of Quiet Influence

You don't have to raise your voice, prove your worth, or out-hustle the world. When your energy is clear, you *are* the influence. People trust you more. Conversations soften. Solutions show up. You feel stronger not because you forced anything—but because you aligned with the moment.

That's the shift.

From chaos to clarity.
From reaction to influence.
From nowhere to **Now Here.**

Let your energy arrive before your words do.
Let your presence speak before your plan does.
Let your stillness do what force never could.

REFLECTION QUESTIONS

Think of a recent moment when you acted impulsively.
What energy were you carrying at the time?

What would have changed if you paused, took a breath, and
chose presence before acting?

What types of energy (fear, frustration, control, love,
service) are most often behind your actions?

Where in your life could you begin practicing "energy first,
action second" today?

How do others experience you when you're fully present
and energetically grounded?

CHAPTER 8

GROUNDED IN THE STORM

"Peace isn't the absence of chaos. It's the presence of you, fully rooted, even in the storm."

STAYING PRESENT WHEN IT MATTERS MOST

It's easy to be mindful when everything's going your way.

When life feels peaceful, when your to-do list is short, when the people around you are kind, and your bank account is full—presence feels natural. You're calm. You breathe deeper. You feel good.

But the real test of presence isn't in the calm.
It's in the chaos.

It's in the middle of a heated conversation, when you're being misunderstood and your heart rate is climbing.

It's when life throws something at you that you didn't ask for—a diagnosis, a betrayal, a loss.

It's in the moment when fear creeps in and whispers old stories, telling you you're not safe, not enough, not in control.

That's when presence matters most.
Because presence isn't just about peace.
It's about power.

The Emotional Earthquake

When I was going through the darkest time in my life—when the pain was physical, emotional, and deeply spiritual—I didn't need motivational quotes or another to-do list. I needed something to *anchor me*. Because everything else felt like it was shaking.

That season broke something in me, but it also built something in me.

I learned that pain, as unbearable as it feels, doesn't mean you've failed. It means you're alive.

And in those moments, the only thing that saved me—was presence.

Not numbing.
Not fixing.
Not escaping.

Just being there.
In the moment.
With the breath.
With the pain.
Without the judgment.

I had to stop running from my discomfort and start *staying* with it. And what I found in those moments was something I had never really known: **groundedness.**

Presence as Your Anchor

Think of presence as an anchor in a storm. The winds may howl. The waves may rise. But if your anchor is secure, you may sway—but you won't drift.

When you're grounded in presence, you no longer get swept away by every thought, every emotion, every external trigger. You become the observer of the storm—not the victim of it.

That doesn't mean you won't feel things deeply. Quite the opposite. It means you'll **feel them fully, without letting them define you.**

Let's be clear—presence doesn't mean perfection. It doesn't mean you won't feel fear, anger, or sadness. It means you won't **become** those things. You won't get lost in them. You won't build your identity around the storm.

You'll remain *you*—still, aware, breathing.

What Being Grounded Looks Like in Real Life

Let me paint a picture.

You're in the middle of an argument. Your old pattern would be to interrupt, raise your voice, defend yourself. But instead, you pause. You feel your feet on the ground. You take one breath— just one—and remind yourself, *"I don't have to react. I can choose how I show up right now."*

That's grounded.

Or maybe you get some bad news. Something that shakes your world. The old you would immediately spiral, assume the worst, try to control everything. But instead, you sit. You let the feelings rise. You cry. You breathe. You stay present with yourself. You don't run.

That's grounded.

Or maybe you're overwhelmed, a hundred things pulling at you, and the pressure to keep it all together is mounting. But instead of pushing harder, you stop. You ask, *"Where is my energy right now? What do I actually need?"* You realign. You return to *now.*

That's grounded.

These moments don't make headlines. But they **change lives.** Because in those moments, you aren't ruled by fear, or ego, or trauma—you are led by presence.

Why the Storm Feels So Loud

The reason so many of us fall apart under pressure is because we've built our identity on things that can be taken. Titles. Roles. Outcomes. Opinions. Control.

But presence doesn't depend on any of that.
It depends on your **awareness**—of this moment, this breath, this choice.

And the beautiful thing is, no one can take that from you. No one can rob you of your breath. Your stillness. Your presence. It's yours, and it's always available.

When you're grounded in who you are—not who others need you to be—chaos doesn't knock you down the same way.
You still feel it, yes.
But you stand in it differently.

You don't react out of fear.
You respond from strength.

Building Emotional Grounding: A Practice

This isn't just a mindset shift—it's a daily practice. Here are a few ways I teach others (and remind myself) to stay grounded in difficult moments:

1. Feel Your Body: The moment emotions rise, return to your body. Place your hand on your chest. Feel your feet on the ground. Engage your senses—smell, touch, sound. The body is *always* in the present. The mind is what wanders.

2. Name What You're Feeling: When you're in pain or triggered, say it out loud or write it down.
"I'm feeling anger. I'm feeling fear. I'm feeling lost."
Labeling it gives you space. And space gives you power.

3. Don't Rush the Exit: Most people feel an emotion and immediately try to fix it or escape it.

Stay with it. Breathe through it. Let the emotion move through you, not become you.

4. Ask Grounding Questions
- "What is true right now?"
- "What can I influence in this moment?"
- "What does this emotion want to teach me?"

5. Use Grounding Mantras: Repeat to yourself:
"I am here. I am safe. I am steady."
"I don't need to control this—I just need to stay present."

When Presence Hurts First… But Heals Always

Let's not pretend that presence is always comfortable. Sometimes being fully present feels like ripping open a wound you've spent years covering.

But here's the truth: presence **hurts before it heals**.
Because it asks you to feel what you've avoided.
To see what you've suppressed.
To be with what's real instead of what's convenient.

But in that raw, unfiltered space—you find your strength.
You meet yourself.
And you realize… you've always had what you needed.

Not in some future version of you.
Not after the storm passes.
But now. Here.

REFLECTION QUESTIONS

1. What is your typical response when life feels chaotic or uncertain?

2. Can you identify a recent moment where you reacted instead of responding? How would presence have changed that moment?

3. What are the "anchors" in your life that help you stay grounded when emotions rise?

4. What would it look like to build a daily practice of presence, even for just five minutes?

5. In what areas of life do you most need to remain grounded in the storm right now?

CHAPTER 9

PRESENCE IN RELATIONSHIPS

"*The most healing thing you can offer another isn't advice—it's your undivided presence.*"

SEEING OTHERS BEGINS WITH BEING HERE

Relationships are where our presence—or lack of it—is most exposed.

You can read every book on communication, learn all the clever phrases, and practice emotional intelligence in theory—but if you're not present with someone, they feel it. They may not be able to name it, but they know when you're not really there. Your body might be across the table, but your mind is miles away.

And that absence?
It's louder than your words.

We've all experienced it. You're talking to someone and you can tell they're only half-listening. They're thinking about how they'll respond, checking their phone, or nodding on autopilot. It leaves you feeling unheard, unseen, unimportant.

Now flip the mirror.

How often are we the ones doing that?
How often do we check out of a moment because we're preoccupied, distracted, or already forming a judgment?

Presence is more than attention—it's **energetic engagement**. It's the quality of your awareness. It's your ability to be here—

not to fix or control, but to witness, feel, and respond from a deeper place of understanding.

And in our most meaningful relationships—romantic, parental, professional, or friendships—presence is the **foundation of trust**.

The Pain of Emotional Absence

There's a unique kind of pain that comes not from arguments or betrayal—but from **emotional absence**. When someone you care about is physically present but emotionally distant, it creates a disconnect that can be hard to explain, but impossible to ignore.

It's the child speaking to a distracted parent.
It's the partner opening up and getting a surface-level "uh-huh" in response.
It's the friend going through pain and receiving advice instead of empathy.

The people in our lives don't need us to be perfect—they need us to be **present**.

When someone is fully with you, even in silence, it heals. It softens the edges. It opens a space where trust can breathe.

But we've become too addicted to multitasking and mental noise to offer that space. We're too busy preparing what we'll say, proving our point, or waiting for our turn to speak. In doing so, we miss what's actually being said—beneath the words.

What Presence Looks Like in Relationships

Presence in relationships doesn't mean you agree with everything or never get frustrated. It means you **show up consciously**.

Here's what that looks like:

- **You listen with your whole self**—not just your ears.

- **You make eye contact**, letting the person know you're here and not somewhere else in your mind.

- **You pause before reacting**, choosing your energy before your words.

- **You hold space**—not to fix, but to allow.

When you're present with someone, they feel safe. Not because you've solved their problem, but because they're not alone in it. That's what changes people. That's what creates connection.

From Defensiveness to Openness

So many of our relationship issues stem from reactivity.

We feel misunderstood, so we snap back.
We feel criticized, so we defend.
We feel hurt, so we shut down.

But what if, instead of reacting, we practiced being present with what we were feeling—*and* with the other person's experience?

It doesn't mean we abandon boundaries. It means we respond from grounded awareness rather than ego-driven fear.

You don't have to be right to be present.
You just have to be *real*.

The most powerful thing you can offer in any relationship isn't advice—it's presence.
It says, "I see you. I hear you. I'm here with you."

That offering alone can soften defensiveness, dissolve arguments, and repair years of disconnection.

One Moment Changed Everything

I remember a conversation with someone I love where I almost repeated an old pattern. We were disagreeing. I felt myself getting defensive, wanting to interrupt and make my point.

But I paused. I took one deep breath. I reminded myself: *Influence starts with energy, not argument.*

Instead of speaking, I stayed silent for a moment and actually listened.

And I didn't just hear their words—I heard their *pain*.
It wasn't about the issue. It was about feeling unseen.
And in that moment, everything shifted.

That breath bought me presence.
That presence changed the entire dynamic.

What could have been a blow-up became a breakthrough.

That's the power of presence. Not just in avoiding conflict, but in transforming it.

Why We Struggle with Presence in Relationships

Presence makes us vulnerable. It requires us to put down our defenses, drop our agenda, and truly feel. And let's be honest—that can be scary.

Sometimes, we avoid presence with others because we've avoided it with ourselves. We don't want to feel our own discomfort, so we numb, deflect, or distract in conversations too.

To be present with someone else, you must first be present with *you*.
You have to feel your own reactions without being ruled by them. You have to meet yourself in compassion before you can offer it to others.

This is why mindfulness isn't just about *you*—it affects every relationship you're in. When you do the inner work of presence, everyone around you benefits.

Practical Tools to Deepen Relational Presence

You don't need to master this overnight. Start with simple practices:

1. Put the Phone Away: When someone is speaking to you, put your phone down. Look them in the eye. Show them they matter.

2. Breathe Before You Speak: When tensions rise, pause and breathe. Let the emotion pass through you before responding. Don't let your ego lead the conversation.

3. Reflect What You Hear: Say back what you're hearing:
"It sounds like you feel…"
"What I'm hearing is…"
"Is this what you're trying to say?"

This shows presence and prevents assumptions.

4. Ask Instead of Assume: Curiosity is presence in action. Instead of reacting, ask, "Can you help me understand?" or "What do you need right now?"

5. Create Sacred Spaces: Set aside time to connect without distractions—at dinner, during a walk, or in bed before sleep. A few minutes of pure presence often means more than hours of physical proximity.

Healing Through Presence

Many broken relationships aren't the result of betrayal—they're the result of neglect. Not intentional harm, but **unintentional absence**.

If there's distance in your relationships, presence is the bridge back.

Show up. Even if you don't have the perfect words. Even if you're afraid. Even if the other person doesn't respond right away.

Let your energy say what your words can't:
"I'm here. I'm with you. I'm not running."

REFLECTION QUESTIONS

1. When was the last time you felt truly seen and heard by someone? What made that moment different?

2. In which of your relationships do you tend to check out or become reactive?

3. What personal discomforts or fears keep you from being fully present with others?

4. How would your closest relationship change if you practiced presence daily?

5. What's one thing you can do today to offer someone your full attention and presence?

CHAPTER 10

PURPOSE OVER PRODUCTIVITY

"You weren't born to prove your worth through output. You were born to embody purpose through presence."

PRESENCE ISN'T A PAUSE —IT'S THE PATH

We live in a world obsessed with productivity.

Everywhere you turn, someone's measuring their worth by how much they got done. How many hours they worked. How many checkboxes they filled in. How many likes, comments, and metrics they accumulated in the name of "progress."

But let me ask you something…

Have you ever been busy all day and still gone to bed feeling empty?

That's the trap.
We confuse movement with meaning.
We mistake effort for alignment.
We believe that our value comes from how much we do instead of *how we show up in what we do.*

Don't get me wrong—discipline, commitment, and work ethic matter. But they're not the same as purpose. You can climb the mountain of success and still feel unfulfilled if you weren't present for the journey. You can accomplish great things but completely miss yourself in the process.

Because purpose isn't found in your output.
It's discovered in your **presence.**

The Danger of Chasing Without Checking In

Many of the people I coach aren't unhappy because they lack talent, goals, or drive. They're exhausted because they've been chasing something they can't define. They're always doing—but rarely being. Always achieving—but rarely arriving.

And when we unpack what's going on, it usually comes back to one simple truth:

They've lost connection to *why* they're doing what they're doing.

When presence disappears, purpose gets hijacked by ego, fear, or external validation. You start running toward something that may not even be meant for you.

And before you know it, you're living someone else's dream.
Building someone else's version of success.
Following a path that leads to burnout, not belonging.

My Own Redefinition of Purpose

For years, I believed purpose was tied to career and productivity. As long as I was working hard, helping others, and staying busy, I thought I was doing what I was meant to do.

But then came the collapse—the dark season I've shared in earlier chapters. The pain. The silence. The dismantling of everything I thought made me valuable. My career shifted. My identity unraveled. And for a while, I didn't know who I was without my role, my output, or my goals.

That was terrifying.
But it was also necessary.

Because in that quiet space, I met something I had avoided for years: **me**.
Not the performer. Not the producer. Not the "motivated" version. Just the presence behind all of it.

And that presence? It was purposeful without doing anything.

That realization changed everything.

The Power of Being vs. Doing

There's a different kind of power that comes from being fully where you are.

It's the moment a father kneels down and looks his child in the eyes, instead of checking his phone.

It's the quiet choice to really listen to a friend's pain without rushing to fix it.

It's the space between breaths when you remember, *"I'm here. And that's enough right now."*

These moments are rich with purpose—not because they're loud or visible, but because they're real.

We've been trained to believe that the more we do, the more we matter. But presence breaks that illusion. Presence says:

"You matter because you exist—not because of your resume."

And when you show up for life—not just as a worker, achiever, or fixer, but as a conscious human being—you bring purpose into everything you touch.

Realigning with Purpose through Presence

So how do we shift from the productivity trap into purposeful living?

Here are a few guiding steps:

1. Slow Down the Doing: The first step is often the hardest. It requires courage to slow down when the world says, "speed up." It takes faith to pause and trust that you're still valuable even when you're not producing something.

Practice taking intentional pauses throughout your day:

- Before a meeting, take one minute to breathe.
- Between tasks, check in with your energy.
- At the end of the day, ask: *Did I live today—or just perform it?*

2. Redefine Success: Instead of measuring success by what you accomplished, try asking:

- Was I present?
- Did I align with my values?
- Did I serve someone from a place of love?
- Did I make space for what matters?

These questions lead to a life you *feel*, not just manage.

3. Infuse Purpose into the Present: You don't need to quit your job or move to the mountains to find purpose. It's already here. The key is infusing intention into what you're doing—whatever that may be.

Washing dishes can become a moment of gratitude.
Driving to work can become a space for reflection.
Holding someone's hand can become an act of healing.
Presence turns ordinary moments into sacred ones.

Purpose Is Found, Not Forced

You don't *force* purpose. You discover it.
And the discovery happens **in the stillness**, in the spaces where you stop trying to prove something and start listening to the deeper voice inside you.

The more present you are, the clearer that voice becomes.
The more aligned your actions become.
And the more peace you find—not because everything's perfect, but because you're finally living *on purpose*.

Not someone else's version of it.
Yours.

One Client's Story: From Burnout to Belonging

I once worked with a high-achieving executive who had reached the top of her field—and felt completely hollow. Every goal checked off her list gave her less joy than the one before it.

When we started our coaching, she kept saying, "I just want to feel like I'm doing something meaningful."

But when I asked what gave her that feeling, she paused. She didn't know.

We began working not on new goals—but on new awareness. I taught her how to reconnect with the present moment. How to ask herself daily: *"Am I acting from alignment or expectation?"* She slowed down. She simplified. She reconnected with her body, her breath, and her own intuition.

She didn't change jobs.
She changed how she *showed up* in the job.

She stopped proving.
She started being.

And in that shift, her energy changed. Her leadership changed. Her life changed.

That's the quiet revolution of presence.
It's not flashy. But it's real. And it's lasting.

REFLECTION QUESTIONS

1. What does "success" mean to you right now—and is that definition aligned with your truth?

2. Where in your life are you doing more than being?

3. Can you recall a moment recently where you were present and it felt deeply purposeful, even if it was simple?

4. What would it feel like to let go of productivity as your identity and anchor into presence instead?

5. What small practice can you adopt today to infuse more intention and presence into your daily life?

CHAPTER 11

A NEW WAY TO LIVE

*"You don't find fulfillment by
chasing more. You find it by arriving fully
in what's already here."*

NOWHERE IS WHERE LIFE BEGINS

If you've made it this far, you've already begun to feel it—that shift.

Maybe it's subtle. Maybe it's still hard to explain.
But something inside you is changing. Not because you've learned something new, but because you're remembering something you've always known:

You were never going nowhere.
You were just never *Now Here.*

And now? Now you're waking up.

You're starting to see that the peace, clarity, and strength you've been searching for weren't waiting for you somewhere out there in the distance. They were right here—in the breath, in the pause, in the presence you had forgotten.

This chapter is not the end. It's the beginning.
Because once you understand the power of presence, you have a choice:
You can keep dipping your toes into it, or you can build your life around it.

And that's what this chapter is about—**a new way to live.**

From Temporary State to Permanent Shift

Many people treat presence like a temporary escape. They meditate to "feel better." They pause when they're overwhelmed. They breathe only when they're drowning.

But presence isn't a break from life.
It *is* life.

It's not a trick you pull out when things get hard. It's a foundation you build so that when things get hard, you're already grounded. Already anchored. Already whole.

The goal is not to have a few present moments.
It's to live *as* presence.

That doesn't mean you float through life in silence.
It means you live with full awareness, intention, and integrity.
It means you bring your whole self into every experience—even the messy ones.

Presence Makes Ordinary Life Extraordinary

We're taught to chase peak moments—vacations, achievements, milestones. But the truth is, life isn't lived in the peaks. It's lived in the in-between.

The quiet moments.
The small conversations.
The choices you make when no one's watching.

And when you are truly present for those moments, they stop feeling small.
They become sacred.

- Washing the dishes becomes an act of gratitude.

- Saying goodbye to a loved one becomes a
  deeper connection.

- Driving in silence becomes a moment of reflection
  and calm.

- Even brushing your teeth becomes a ritual, not a routine.

Presence elevates everything.
Not because it changes what you do—but because it transforms **how you do it.**

What a Life of Presence Looks Like

Let me paint a picture of what this can look like—not as an ideal, but as a daily practice:

You wake up and before reaching for your phone, you reach for your breath. You place your hand on your chest and feel your aliveness. You start the day not with anxiety, but with **awareness**.

You go about your morning with mindfulness—feeling the water on your skin, noticing the taste of your coffee, honoring the silence or the sound.

When challenges arise, you don't automatically react. You pause. You choose your energy before your actions. You ask, *"What does this moment require from me, not just what do I want from it?"*

You speak slower. Listen deeper. Move more intentionally.
You become aware of your patterns and gently shift them.
You give others your presence—not your performance.
You create space between stimulus and response.

And most importantly, you *remember who you are*—not the roles you play or the goals you chase, but the **being behind all the doing.**

That is living **NowHere.**

Living with Less Noise, More Knowing

Presence quiets the noise—externally and internally.
And in that silence, you start hearing something far more valuable: **your own truth.**

You begin to trust your intuition again.
You sense when something's off—not because you overthink it, but because you *feel* it.
You align your actions with your values.
You say no to what drains you.
You say yes to what expands you.
You stop abandoning yourself for approval.
You begin to live from **inside out**, not outside in.

The result?
You may still face storms, but you're no longer drowning.
You may still get triggered, but you recover faster.
You may still feel fear, but it no longer dictates your choices.

You stop chasing your life.
You begin to *experience* it.

From Reaction to Creation

When you live in presence, you become a **creator** again—not a reactor.

You create your energy.
You create your response.
You create your reality—not because you control the world, but because you influence your experience of it.

And that influence?
It's how you begin to change your life, one conscious breath at a time.

A Personal Practice: My Return to Presence

For me, this journey didn't begin with a grand spiritual awakening. It started with pain. With hitting bottom. With losing myself in roles, expectations, and the lie that I had to do more to be more.

But in that pain, something cracked open.

And through that crack, light started coming in.

I started slowing down.
I started questioning everything I believed about success, worth, and control.
I started listening—not to the noise of the world, but to the still, steady voice inside me that whispered:

You are not going nowhere. You are Now Here. Start from there.

And that's where everything changed—not because life got easier, but because I got more aware. More rooted. More real.

That is available to you, too. Right now. Right here.

Your Invitation

You don't need to quit your job, move to a retreat center, or escape the world to live this way.

You just need to **return to presence**.
And then return again. And again. And again.

Until it's no longer something you practice—but who you are.

Let your life be the practice.
Let your presence be your power.
Let the *Now Here* be your home.

Because from this place… everything begins.

REFLECTION QUESTIONS

1. What does "living present" mean to you—and how is it different from how you've been living?

2. Where in your daily routine could you slow down and bring more awareness?

3. What distractions or patterns most often pull you out of the present moment?

4. What's one ritual or habit you can create to ground your mornings in presence?

5. If you chose to live "NowHere" starting today, what would shift immediately in your relationships, energy, or decisions?

CHAPTER 12

THE QUIET REVOLUTION OF PRESENCE

"You were never lost—you were simply waiting to arrive in the only place that ever mattered: Now Here."

If you're still here reading these words, then something inside you already knows the truth:

You are not broken.
You are not behind.
You are not going nowhere.

You're simply waking up.

And that waking up is not loud or dramatic. It's subtle. It's sacred. It happens slowly—moment by moment—as you begin to return to yourself. Not the version of you the world shaped. Not the version you perform for others. But the one beneath all of that. The one that's always been **Now Here**.

Throughout this book, we've walked together through the fog of distraction, the illusion of control, the lies of productivity, and the pain of reactivity. We've stood together in the storm. And each chapter has been a step toward the same truth: **presence is the foundation of freedom.**

Not external freedom—the kind the world sells you.
But inner freedom—the kind no one can give or take from you.

That freedom begins the moment you stop chasing life and start *experiencing* it.

What You've Reclaimed

Presence isn't a trend. It's not a trick. It's not just for yogis or monks or people with time on their hands.

It's for the real world.
It's for busy people.
For overwhelmed parents.
For driven leaders.
For anxious teens.
For anyone who's ever felt lost and is finally ready to come home.

And when you begin to live NowHere, you begin to reclaim what was never gone—just forgotten:

- **Your energy**, no longer scattered by overthinking or regret.
- **Your awareness**, no longer dulled by distraction or reaction.
- **Your influence**, no longer hijacked by fear or ego.
- **Your relationships**, no longer weakened by absence or performance.
- **Your purpose**, no longer confused with productivity or perfection.

What you've reclaimed... is *you*.

The Illusion is Over

You were never supposed to live in a cycle of rushing, doubting, proving, and controlling. That's a lie we've been fed by a world that values image over inner truth.

But now, you see the illusion for what it is.

Control? It was never real.
Certainty? It was never promised.
Fulfillment? It was never out there.

It was always in the **moment**.
In the **breath**.
In the **stillness** you kept avoiding.
In the **life** you were too distracted to live.

Now you know.
Now you feel it.
Now, you are here.

And that's where all your power has been waiting.

Your Influence Begins Here

You cannot influence anything if you're not present. You cannot love deeply, speak clearly, or decide wisely if you are not **here**.

Presence isn't just the path to peace—it's the path to **impact**.

As you go back into your daily life, the world won't slow down for you. People will still frustrate you. Triggers will still try to hook you. Life will still throw curveballs.

But now, you have something different.
You have awareness.
You have choice.
You have tools.

You don't have to respond the way you used to.
You don't have to live in fear, rush, or reactivity.
You don't have to fix, force, or flee.

You can pause.
You can breathe.
You can show up on purpose.
And that one decision will shift everything around you—even when nothing else changes.

This Is the Revolution

We're not changing the world by shouting louder.
We're changing it by showing up more clearly. More grounded. More awake. More compassionate.

You want to change your life?
Start by being **here** for it.

You want to heal the past?
Stop replaying it. Start replacing it—with presence, awareness, and aligned energy.

You want to love deeply?
Stop waiting for the right moment. *Be* the moment. Be the space where others feel safe enough to be themselves.

This is the revolution.
It's quiet.
It's conscious.
It's personal.
And it starts with you.

Right now.

What Happens Now

This isn't the kind of book you finish and shelve.

This is a way of living you return to—daily, hourly, breath by breath.

There will be days you forget. Days you react. Days you check out. That's okay.
Presence isn't about being perfect.
It's about coming back.
Over and over again.

No judgment.
No shame.
Just the gentle, honest practice of saying:

"I'm here now. Let's begin again."

Let your life become a living reflection of that practice. Let the way you walk, speak, rest, and engage all be infused with that quiet, powerful knowing:

I am Now Here. And that is enough.

You Are the Message

There's no need to memorize every chapter or master every tool. The point of this book was never to give you answers. It was to help you *remember* who you are and where you've always belonged.

Presence isn't just something you do.
It becomes who you are.
And when you live that way, your life becomes the message.

Not your accomplishments.
Not your schedule.
Not your ability to explain or prove anything.

Your energy will say what your words cannot.
Your stillness will become safety for others.
Your authenticity will awaken others to their own.

And that?
That's how we change everything—without needing to control anything.

A Final Word: Come Home

There's a voice inside you that knows when you're home.

It's not the voice that shouts when you've achieved something.
It's not the one that judges your performance.
It's the quiet one that whispers when you slow down enough to listen.

It says:

"You've been looking out there for so long. But I've been here, waiting.
You were never lost.
You were just not here yet.
Now... you are.
Welcome home."

This is *The Power of NowHere*.
It's yours now.

Live it.
Share it.
Be it.

30-DAY PRESENCE CHALLENGE

A DAILY RETURN TO NOWHERE

This isn't a checklist. This is a commitment.

A commitment to meet your life as it is.
To stop chasing clarity and start choosing it.
To embody presence not just when it's easy—but when it's needed most.

Each day, choose *intention over autopilot*. Breathe. Reflect. Slow down. Notice. Return.
Presence isn't about escaping life—it's about **re-entering it fully**.

Let's begin.

WEEK 1: Coming Back to Now

Theme: Reconnecting with the Present Moment

Day 1 – Breathe First
Before reaching for your phone in the morning, place one hand on your chest. Take five conscious breaths. Remind yourself: *"I'm now here."*

Day 2 – One Task, Full Attention
Choose one ordinary task (eating, brushing your teeth, washing dishes) and give it your full, undivided attention. Feel every motion. Be fully present.

Day 3 – Pause Before You React

Today, when something triggers you, pause. Take a breath. Ask: *"What energy do I want to respond with?"*

Day 4 – 3-Minute Stillness

Set a timer. Sit in silence for 3 minutes. No music. No talking. Just your breath. Let discomfort come. Let clarity rise.

Day 5 – Where Am I Now?

Throughout your day, ask yourself: *"Where am I—mentally, emotionally, physically?"* This check-in realigns you with the present.

Day 6 – Device-Free Hour

Set aside one hour today without your phone, computer, or TV. Observe how your mind and body feel when not being pulled elsewhere.

Day 7 – Reflect & Journal

What did you notice about yourself this week? When did you feel most present? When did you disconnect?

WEEK 2: Presence in Relationships

Theme: Showing Up for Others with Awareness

Day 8 – Look People in the Eye

In every interaction today—whether at home or work—offer eye contact and stillness. Let them feel seen.

Day 9 – Ask, Don't Assume

Instead of reacting or advising, ask a loved one: *"What do you need right now?"* Listen. Be fully there.

Day 10 – No Multitasking Conversations

When someone speaks to you today, put everything else down. Offer your undivided attention—even for 60 seconds.

Day 11 – Presence Over Performance

Today, don't try to impress. Just connect. Be authentic. Let people meet the *real* you.

Day 12 – Appreciate Without Agenda

Send a message, write a note, or speak directly to someone and express appreciation—without expecting anything in return.

Day 13 – Respond With Intention

In moments of tension, practice conscious responding. Breathe. Soften your tone. Focus on connection over correction.

Day 14 – Reflect & Journal

What shifted in your relationships this week when you were more present? How did you feel being seen—and seeing others?

WEEK 3: Anchoring Your Energy

Theme: Choosing Your Energy Before Action

Day 15 – Energy Check-In

At three points today (morning, midday, evening), pause and ask:

THE POWER OF NOWHERE

"What energy am I carrying?"
"Is this how I want to show up?"

Day 16 – Walk in Silence
Take a 10- to 20-minute walk without your phone or headphones. Let your senses lead the experience.

Day 17 – Label the Emotion
When emotions rise, name them without judgment:
"This is frustration."
"This is fear."
Let naming create space.

Day 18 – Say No Mindfully
Today, say no to something that drains you or pulls you away from your values. Protect your energy.

Day 19 – Create a Grounding Ritual
Light a candle. Sit in silence. Read a passage. Pray. Breathe. Choose something simple to root yourself in presence today.

Day 20 – Do Nothing for 10 Minutes
Let go of productivity. No agenda. No outcome. Just sit, lie down, or be still. Let yourself *be*.

Day 21 – Reflect & Journal
How did your energy shift this week? When did you feel most grounded? What helped you return when you drifted?

WEEK 4: Embodying Presence as a Way of Life

Theme: Making Presence Your Default, Not the Exception

Day 22 – Begin With Awareness
Before starting your day, sit quietly for 3 minutes. Set the tone. Ask: *"How do I want to show up today?"*

Day 23 – Let It Be Imperfect
Catch yourself trying to force or perfect something today. Instead, pause and allow the moment to be enough as it is.

Day 24 – Watch Your Self-Talk
Notice your inner dialogue today. Would you speak that way to a friend? Replace judgment with compassion.

Day 25 – Digital Sunset
Turn off all screens one hour before bed. Be with your thoughts. Let your mind settle naturally.

Day 26 – Serve from Presence
Offer your presence as a gift. Help someone without rushing or fixing—just be with them. Witness them.

Day 27 – Reclaim the "In-Between" Moments
Be mindful during transitions—walking to your car, waiting in line, brushing your hair. Use these as cues to return to presence.

Day 28 – Revisit Your Why

Reflect on your purpose. What matters to you most? Are your actions aligned with your values?

Day 29 – Choose Peace Over Proof
In a moment of conflict, choose inner peace over being right. Let your groundedness speak louder than ego.

Day 30 – Reflect, Celebrate, Continue
Journal: What has changed in you? What did you reclaim? What will you continue?
You didn't just complete a challenge—you returned home to yourself.

Final Words

Presence is not a moment. It's not something you check off. It's the **lens** you live through. The energy you bring. The truth you embody.

Keep returning. Keep listening. Keep living **NowHere**.

Because this isn't the end of the challenge.
It's the beginning of a life that feels real again.

DAILY AWARENESS PROMPTS

RECLAIM PRESENCE.
CHOOSE ENERGY.
LIVE NOWHERE.

These prompts are **anchors** for your awareness. Use them to return to your breath, your truth, and your influence. Each one is a small door back to *Now Here*.

How to Use These Prompts

WHERE to use them:

- During transitions (before a meeting, during a drive, walking into your home)

- In moments of emotional tension or mental clutter

- At set times (wake-up, lunch, end of day)

- During repetitive or mundane activities (brushing teeth, walking, doing dishes)

WHEN to use them:

- Anytime you feel anxious, rushed, reactive, or disconnected

- When you're about to make a decision or engage in a conversation

- When you're slipping into autopilot or distraction

- When you're judging, avoiding, or controlling

HOW to use them:

- Silently reflect or speak them aloud

- Write them in a journal or use them as phone reminders

- Let the answer *guide your next breath—not just your next action*

- Pause long enough to feel the shift—don't just rush past the insight

PROMPTS + PURPOSE + EXAMPLES

"Where am I right now?"

Purpose: Reclaim mental presence and bring yourself into alignment

Why it matters: Most people live in the past or future. This pulls you back to *now*.

Use when: You realize you're distracted, overthinking, or emotionally spiraling.

Example: You're driving but thinking about a stressful conversation from yesterday.
Ask: *"Where am I right now?"*
Answer: *Driving. Safe. Sunlight on my face. I'm okay.*
Result: You return to the present.

"What energy am I bringing into this moment?"

Purpose: Realign your internal state before speaking, acting, or deciding

Why it matters: Energy precedes outcome. Your presence affects results.

Use when: Entering a meeting, a family conversation, or facing conflict.

Example: Before picking up the phone to call your partner during tension:
Ask: *"Am I bringing anxiety, love, or control into this?"*
Result: You breathe, soften, and choose a different energy.

"Am I reacting... or responding?"

Purpose: Pause automatic behavior and reclaim influence

Why it matters: Reaction is unconscious. Response is mindful

Use when: You feel defensive, irritated, or impulsive.

Example: Someone criticizes your work. Instead of snapping...
Ask: "Is this a reaction... or can I choose a response?"
Result: You breathe, regulate, and lead with maturity instead of ego.

"What's real right now?"

Purpose: Detach from imagined fears or stories

Why it matters: Most suffering comes from resisting what is or imagining what isn't.

Use when: You're caught in anxiety, catastrophizing, or what-if loops.

Example: You're worried your friend hasn't texted back.
Ask: *"What's real right now?"*
Answer: *They haven't responded. That's all. Everything else is a story.*
Result: Anxiety reduces, presence returns.

"What does this moment need from me?"

Purpose: Shift from ego to intention

Why it matters: Ego says, "what do *I* want from this?" Presence asks, "what can I *bring* to this?"

Use when: You're tempted to push your agenda or prove something.

Example: During a work presentation, you feel pressure to impress.
Ask: *"What does this moment need from me?"*
Answer: *Clarity. Calm. Honesty. Not performance.*
Result: You embody integrity, not image.

"Can I allow this moment to be what it is?"

Purpose: Reduce resistance and control

Why it matters: Suffering intensifies when we resist reality.

Use when: You're frustrated, rushing, or judging what's happening.

Example: You're stuck in traffic and feel rising anger.
Ask: *"Can I allow this moment to be what it is?"*
Answer: *Yes, I don't control the traffic. But I control my energy.*
Result: Peace, even if the circumstances stay the same.

"Is this aligned or automatic?"

Purpose: Bring intention into your decisions

Why it matters: You can be busy and completely unaligned.

Use when: You're about to say yes, start a project, or take on a commitment.

Example: Someone asks you for a favor. You instinctively want to say yes.
Ask: *"Is this aligned with my energy, time, and values?"*
Result: You pause, and maybe say no—with peace, not guilt.

"What part of me needs compassion right now?"

Purpose: Build internal presence and self-awareness

Why it matters: Inner conflict can't heal through judgment.

Use when: You're being hard on yourself, feeling shame, or spiraling into old patterns.

Example: You forgot something important and feel deep guilt.
Ask: *"What part of me needs compassion right now?"*
Answer: *The part that still thinks perfection equals worth.*
Result: You offer grace instead of punishment.

"Do I need to fix this... or just feel this?"

Purpose: Break the cycle of control and suppression

Why it matters: Some pain just needs presence—not solutions.

Use when: You're uncomfortable and rushing to distract or numb.

Example: You feel grief surfacing. You reach for your phone to scroll. Pause.
Ask: *"Do I need to fix this... or feel this?"*
Result: You stay with the emotion. You let it move through. Healing begins.

"What am I grateful for in this exact moment?"

Purpose: Expand presence through appreciation

Why it matters: Gratitude anchors you in what's real and enough.

Use when: You feel overwhelmed, discouraged, or mentally scattered.

Example: You're frustrated by how much is left on your plate. Pause.
Ask: *"What can I be grateful for right now?"*
Answer: *This breath. This home. My ability to care.*
Result: Perspective shifts. Peace returns.

FINAL TIPS FOR USING AWARENESS PROMPTS

1. **Pick 1–2 prompts per week** and use them consistently.

2. **Write them on sticky notes** around your home, car, or workspace.

3. **Pair them with anchors** like waking up, brushing your teeth, or taking a break.

4. **Journal your answers** at the end of the day. Not to judge—just to observe and grow.

5. **Speak them aloud** when emotions run high. They help you *interrupt old programming*.

Closing Reminder

You don't need more time. You need *more presence* in the time you already have.

These awareness prompts aren't magic words—they're keys. Each one unlocks the door to the only place your power has ever lived:
Now. Here.

Choose one today. Breathe into it. Let it guide you back to yourself.

ABOUT THE AUTHOR

Mike Jensen II is a Life Performance Coach with over 12 years of experience helping individuals achieve the greatest performance of their lives and live up to their potential. He holds several certifications in Energy Leadership, Mental Toughness Training, Professional Coaching, and the Science of Happiness. Mike writes a daily short blog on various social media platforms under MBR3 Coaching, which has been updated every day for over eight years without fail. His blog focuses on encouraging others to think outside the box, recognize the abundance around them, and choose a different way to live.

When he's not writing or blogging, Mike is coaching clients all over the world. In his personal time, he enjoys spending time with his amazing wife, family, and especially his grandchildren. Although Mike has lived all over the United States, he always returns to Ottawa, Kansas, a small town he loves for its smallness, slowness, and quietness.

Mike has dedicated his life to serving others, helping them find sustainable happiness and live up to their potential. He believes that everyone has a purpose and unlimited potential.

ABOUT THE PUBLISHER

Dear Reader,

As you hold this remarkable book in your hands, we want to express our heartfelt gratitude for becoming a part of the Live Life Happy Community of readers. Your curiosity and thirst for knowledge fuel our passion for publishing meaningful non-fiction works.

At Live Life Happy Publishing, our mission is rooted in bringing forth literature that not only entertains but uplifts, supports, and nourishes the soul. We firmly believe that books have the power to transform lives, to ignite passions, and to spread joy far and wide.

Behind every word, every chapter, lies the dedication of our authors who pour their hearts and souls into their craft. Their ultimate aim? To touch your life in profound ways, to inspire, and to leave an indelible mark on your journey.

Your role in this journey is invaluable; by sharing your thoughts through reviews, spreading the word to others, or reaching out to the authors themselves, you become an integral part of sparking transformation in countless lives, igniting a ripple effect of joy and enlightenment.

And if, perchance, you or someone you know has dreams of writing, of sharing a message, or of unleashing a powerful story unto the world, know that Live Life Happy Publishing stands ready to guide you. Our doors are open, our ears attuned, and our hearts eager to hear your message.

So, dear reader, let us, continue to spread the power of literature, one page at a time. Reach out, share, and most importantly, never underestimate the power of your message to touch lives.

With warmest regards,

LiveLifeHappyPublishing.com

P.S. Remember, books change lives. Whose life will you touch with yours?

www.ingramcontent.com/pod-product-compliance
Lightning Source LLC
LaVergne TN
LVHW051244080426

835513LV00016B/1726